The Literary Gothic
Critical Essays

Marija Elektra Rodriguez

HUNTRESS INK

DEDICATION

This book is dedicated to the memory of my dear friend Ana, who told me many horror stories, all of which were true.

CONTENTS

ACKNOWLEDGMENTS

Thank you to Dr. O'Brien, lecturer of English Literature, for her review and feedback on my criticisms.

Thank you to my family for their ongoing support and love.

1 THE SUPERNATURAL IN GOTHIC NARRATIVES

he supernatural functions as an element of retribution and as a force of justice in gothic narratives, particularly in texts dealing with inappropriate power succession. The mechanism of the supernatural evolved from its origin as an overt, inexplicable phenomenon in Walpole's *The*

Castle of Otranto, into an intellectualized projection of the disturbed mind in Poe's *The Tell Tale Heart*, and as an allegory in *The Fall of the House of Usher*.[1] Walpole's employment of the supernatural is highly politicized. He constructs a tangible, hostile force, with strong religious and pagan overtones, that undermines the institution of tyranny and restores the correct royal bloodline in Otranto. This contrasts Poe's use of the supernatural as a conduit of justice. Poe suggests a psychological origin for the inexplicable elements of his tales and internalizes the paranormal; he uses phonic narratives to mimic the inner fixations of an unstable mind, which

---

[1] This process of intellectualization included the use of the "explained" supernatural by authors such as Radcliff. See Ellis, *History of Gothic Fiction*, pp.66–8.

manifest themselves as theatrical and extraordinary events in his tales. Despite the adaptable nature of the supernatural, it is ultimately used in a similar manner by both authors: as an instrument of justice and retribution that corrects the actions of disturbed individuals.

Walpole's genre-blending novel *The Castle of Otranto* portrays the supernatural as an agency of power and justice that revokes the kingship of Manfred, a usurper, and reinstates Theodore, the legitimate ruler of Otranto. Although the underlying nature of these supernatural events is never explicitly stated, the author alludes to both fate, a pagan force, and Judeo-Christian powers, as circumventing Manfred's will. Manfred's attempted rape of Isabella is interrupted by the animation of a portrait of his ancestor.[2] His initial reaction to this supernatural occurrence is one of horror; he assumes that "the devils themselves" are subverting his will.[3] When he attempts to follow the specter into a chamber he is thwarted by "an invisible hand".[4] The reference to this unseen force has a strong religious connotation, suggesting the "hand of god", a Judeo-Christian motif that dates back to late antiquity.[5] The effect

---

[2] Walpole, *Otranto*, p.26.
[3] Walpole, *Otranto*, p.26.
[4] Walpole, *Otranto*, p.26.
[5] For "hand of god" in Judeo-Christian iconography, see Didron, *Christian Iconography*, pp.45, 55, 97. Andriopoulos discusses the significance of this imagery by exploring Adam Smith's use of the "invisible hand", not only as an economic force, but also as an instrument of the sublime in pagan cultures. Smith suggests that the "terror" associated

of this "invisible hand" is to subvert Manfred's will—the distraction allows Isabella to escape, frustrating Manfred and putting him in direct conflict with supernatural forces. He states, "Since Hell will not satisfy my curiosity ... I will use the human means in my power for preserving my race".[6] This suggests that Manfred believes he is being antagonized by demoniacal forces, causing him to implore the help of "God and his Holy Trinity" to maintain his power.[7] Manfred's self-perception is ultimately misguided; he is stripped of his kingship by the aid of these

---

with a natural phenomenon, such as "thunder and lightning, storms and sunshine", was perceived to be "the invisible hand of Jupiter". See Andriopoulos, *The Invisible Hand*, p.740.

[6] Walpole, *Otranto*, p.26.
[7] Walpole, *Otranto*, p.63.

paranormal forces and retires to a monastery to repent, a form of punishment with strong Catholic overtones. The use of the "Catholicized" supernatural adds a dimension of authority to this paranormal mechanism. By putting the weight of an institution behind his imagery, Walpole is suggesting that the abuse of power, via inappropriate succession, will be punished by supernatural forces, particularly when the law of man does not have the capacity for justice.

Judeo-Christian forces are not the only form of supernatural agents employed by Walpole. The pre-Christian notion of destiny is also alluded to in the text, suggesting that fate and freewill are at odds in the narrative. The death of Conrad, Manfred's only male heir, is propelled by attempts to avoid the cryptic prophecy shrouding the ruling line.[8] It is only through the intervention of the supernatural, in the form of a giant helmet, that Manfred's dynasty is broken. Walpole does not attempt to rationalize the event; Manfred "wished in vain to believe a vision", but he cannot dismiss the possible fulfilment of the oracle as a hallucination, and his continued attempts to avoid the oracle are subverted by supernatural forces.[9] Hippolyta also alludes to her son's death as an act of fate, stating that "there is a destiny hangs over us; the hand of Providence is stretched out".[10] Again the imagery of an

---

[8] Walpole, *Otranto*, p19.

[9] Walpole, *Otranto*, p19.

[10] Walpole, *Otranto*, p.90. Note that Providence may be either Judeo-Christian (Divine Providence) or pagan. In this context, Hippolyta is specifically

"invisible hand" is employed by Walpole; however, in this instance the icon is distinctly pagan and linked to destiny, as opposed to the will of a Judeo-Christian God.[11] Andriopoulous discusses the significance of this destabilizing force, suggesting that the "authorial control" of the narrator is diminished by the supernatural events, which may reflect Walpole's own misgivings about the supernatural in his work.[12]

---

connecting Providence with destiny and the oracle associated with Manfred's dynasty, which has strong pagan overtones. This is in opposition to the Judeo-Christian belief of "God's will". See Vamvacas, *The Founders of Western Thought*, p.10, and Jowers, *Four Views on Divine Providence*, pp.32, 39.

[11] Ambiguous oracles were a key feature of Classical Greek and Roman (pagan) religions, specifically through the institution of the Delphic oracle, which was shut down by the Christian emperor Theodosius I. See Broad, *The Oracle*, p.254.

[12] Andriopoulos, *The Invisible Hand*, p.742. Walpole misdirectingly claims his text as an historical narrative

In his original preface, Walpole apologizes for the supernatural, implying that its employment creates an inferior narrative, and that such embellishments were not the product of his rational age.[13] Walpole makes the conscious decision not only to set his work in the distant past, in a period in which fantastical events were less likely to be ridiculed, but also to set his work in a foreign country, the Kingdom of Naples: the "empire of superstition".[14] By employing this

---

composed during the Middle Ages. See Walpole, *Otranto,* p.5.

[13] Walpole, *Otranto,* p.6.

[14] Walpole, *Otranto,* p.5. There is a prevalence of Romance language cultures in Gothic narratives; for example, many of Radcliff's works are set in either Italy or France, Lewis' *The Monk* and Poe's *The Casque of Amontillado* are set in Spain, many of Poe's work have a French connotation, and Stoker's *Dracula* is partially set in Romania.

historical and geographical setting, Walpole is accessing a period of turmoil in the Catholic Church in which remnants of the pagan past were being forcefully eradicated. Walpole captures the antagonism between the pagan and the Christian by his varied use of the supernatural as an instrument of justice; he blends both types of portents into his narrative, heightening the subtext of retribution against inappropriate succession.

Regardless of whether or not Walpole intended to embed his supernatural forces in either the pagan or Judeo-Christian tradition, it is evident that his text is intensely politicized, as the supernatural is the primary force that removes Manfred as tyrant and reveals Theodore as the rightful heir to the throne. Walpole, who was himself a member of parliament, was writing during a period of English history imbued with anxieties about the legitimacy of power and rebellion.[15] The two centuries preceding Walpole's work had seen drastic social changes, including the establishment of the Church of England, the English Civil War, the Gunpowder Plot and the Glorious Revolution, among many other instances of social upheaval.[16] This internal dynamic of anxiety about constant power struggles provides a core theme in Walpole's

---

[15] Walpole, *Otranto*, p.xi.
[16] Lacey, *English History*, pp.29, 102, 245, 289.

narrative; ultimately it is the rite of ascension to the throne that propels the supernatural occurrences, and Manfred's attempts to escape the prophecy are due to his insecurities about maintaining his tyranny. By including the supernatural as an agent of justice, Walpole is being critical of his own society. He suggests that there is a valid social anxiety concerning the institution of monarchy and the mechanism of conferring power from one generation to another.

The fear of misplaced succession and the use of the supernatural as a means of correcting such misconduct are not limited to the Gothic narratives of eighteenth-century England. Poe also explores the concept of the supernatural as an agent of justice; however, he internalizes the phenomenon as a psychological event.[17] In *The Tell Tale Heart*, the use of the supernatural is very subtle and acts as a means of retribution when succession is forced by murder. Initially, the narrator seems intensely rational; he states that madness has "sharpened" his senses, in particular his ability to hear, which is preternaturally sensitive.[18] It is this keen sensitivity that leads him to murder, which he perceives to be an entirely logical act, in order to rid himself of the

---

[17] The use of the supernatural in the gothic genre had undergone various refinements by the time Poe was composing his works. A key development was Radcliff's "explained supernatural", see Ellis, *History of Gothic Fiction*, pp.66–8.

[18] Poe, *The Complete Tales*, p.303.

disfigured eye of the old man.[19] Although the connection between the old man and narrator is never explicitly divulged, it bears resemblance to a filial relationship. The narrator states, "I loved the old man ... for his gold I had no desire", implying that there is a familial connection between the two.[20] Despite the narrator's affection for his father figure, he desires to be rid of him, and this causes his mind to begin the slow process of deterioration. Poe uses phonic narrative to subtly introduce the supernatural as a

---

[19] The old man's eye is likened to a vulture's, and is described as "pale blue eye, with a film over it". Poe, *The Complete Tales*, p.303. This is particularly suggestive of Sophocles *Oedipus Rex*, a play in which the protagonist's eyes are also mutilated, primarily due to their role as moralizing agents, and as witnesses to inappropriate succession. See Sophocles, *Oedipus Rex*, p.49; Robinson, *Order and Sentience*, pp.78.

[20] Poe, *The Complete Tales*, p.303.

parallel for the narrator's insanity. He portrays the narrator's monomania with regard to a thudding sound via the repetition of the word "louder", which echoes the frenzied beating of a heart.[21] The tempo of the narrative slows during the revelation of this supernatural sound, mimicking the slow decay of the narrator's sanity throughout the recounting of his tale.[22] Ultimately, he confesses his crimes to the police, propelled by

---

[21] Poe, *The Complete Tales*, p.306. Poe also uses this literary effect in other works such as *The Bells*, where the repetition of words mimics the repetition of chiming bells. See Poe, *The Complete Tales*, p.957; Hoffman, *Poe*, p.2.

[22] Around one fifth of the narrative is devoted to this final revelation, 27 out of 159 lines in Poe, *The Complete Tales*, pp.303–6. It is only in the final line of the narrative that the inexplicable noise is revealed to be the thudding of a dead man's heart. This noise is only perceivable to the narrator, suggesting that the supernatural occurrence is actually the workings of his disturbed mind. Poe, *The Complete Tales*, p.306.

what he perceives to be an external supernatural force. In this sense, the supernatural is acting as an internal instrument of justice; although Poe constructs the supernatural event as the projections of an unhinged mind, from the point of view of the narrator, the animated heart is an external act of the paranormal, revealing his culpability and exposing him to the police.

Poe's use of the supernatural as an agent of justice in relation to inappropriate succession is also evident in *The Fall of the House of Usher*. The Gothic motifs of ruins and decay provide an allusion to the distant Usher line, reiterating that the once noble family has deteriorated due to inappropriate—and possibly incestuous—

succession.[23] The narrator imbues the house with human features; he describes "vacant eye-like windows", which suggest that the house is animated and a moral witness to the degradation of the Usher pedigree.[24] This deterioration is implied through the incestuous relationship between Roderick and Madeline, a situation that ultimately leads to a lack of succession and the expiration of the Usher family.[25] The symbolism of the decaying House of Usher, and its ultimate demise, is subject to mixed scholarly debate. Hoffman reads the image as both an allegory for the state of moral and economic decay in the

---

[23] Note that the incest is never explicitly stated, but it is strongly suggested, both in the current generation with Roderick and Madeline, and in the preceding generations. See Hoffman, *Poe*, pp.311–2.
[24] Poe, *The Complete Tales*, p.231.
[25] Hoffman, *Poe*, pp.311–2.

American South during Poe's era, and as a representation of the common, immoral "soul" of the Usher family, diseased by incest.[26] Other scholars, such as Allison, suggest a more psychological symbolism: the house represents the collective Usher psyche, decayed and disturbed by illness and anxiety.[27] Despite the lack of consensus surrounding Poe's underlying symbolism it is ultimately the force of the supernatural that corrects the transgressions of the Usher family upon its ancestors by destroying the once noble and aristocratic house. Poe constructs an allegorical form of supernatural justice; the inexplicable physical collapse of the house parallels the breakdown of the bloodline

---

[26] Hoffman, *Poe,* pp.305; 315–6.

[27] Allison, *Coleridgean,* pp.41–2.

due to inappropriate relationships, which ultimately results in a lack of succession for the Usher dynasty.

The use of the supernatural is a key element in Gothic narratives, and is an important tool for exploring social concerns such as the legitimacy of authority and succession anxiety. Walpole amplifies the prominence of the supernatural as an agency of power and a medium of justice; he uses fantastical creatures and phantasms to dethrone the usurper of Otranto and reinstate the correct bloodline. Poe explores the more mundane instances of succession: an unnamed narrator who murders an older man in *The Tell Tale Heart*, and the lack of succession due to illness and incest in *The Fall of the House of Usher.* In both of these tales, Poe employs a subtle, psychological aspect of the supernatural—as the workings of a disturbed mind or as an allegory for mental anxiety. Both extremes of the supernatural are ultimately used for a similar end: illegitimate or inappropriate succession is punished by paranormal forces acting as instruments of justice. Regardless of the severity of the supernatural, Poe and Walpole both illustrate the intrinsic nature of the paranormal in Gothic narratives as a means of obtaining justice, particularly when human capabilities fall short.

Bibliography

Primary Sources

Poe, E.A., *The Complete Tales and Poems of Edgar Allan Poe* (London: Random House, 1965).

Sophocles, *Oedipus Rex*, trans. Sir George Young (London: Dover Publications, 1991).

Walpole, H., *The Castle of Otranto* (Oxford & London: Oxford University Press, 2008).

Secondary Sources

Allison, J., "Coleridgean Self-Development: Entrapment and Incest in 'The Fall of the House of Usher'" *South Central Review* 5 no.1 (spring, 1988) pp.4–7.

Andriopoulos, S., "The Invisible Hand: Supernatural Agency in Political Economy and the   Gothic Novel" *ELH* 66 no.3 (fall, 1999) pp.739–58.

Broad, W.J., *The Oracle* (London: Penguin Books, 2007).

Didron, M., & Millington, E.J., *Christian Iconography* (Whitefish: Kessinger Publishing, 2007).

Ellis, M., *The History of Gothic Fiction* (Edinburgh: Edinburgh University Press, 2005).

Hoffman, D., *Poe Poe Poe Poe Poe Poe Poe Poe* (New York: Double Day, 1972).

Jowers, D. & Craig, W.L., *Four Views on Divine Providence* (Michigan: Zondervan Publications, 2011).

Lacey, R., *Great Tales from English History* (New York: Little, Brown and Company, 2007).

Robinson, E.A., "Order and Sentience in 'The Fall of the House of Usher'" *PMLA* 76 no.1 (March, 1961) pp.68–81.

Vamvacas, C.J., *The Founders of Western Thought*, trans. Robert Crist (New York: Springer Publishing, 2009).

2 THE "OTHER" IN GOTHIC NARRATIVES

The role of the "other" in Gothic narratives is a recurring source of tension that conveys various underlying social anxieties evident in the Victorian era.[28] Bram Stoker's *Dracula* and Henry James' *The Turn of the Screw* suggest a sense of

---

[28] The concept of the "other", in opposition to the "self", serves as a point of differentiation between two entities. Said discusses the ethnic "other" as a "cultural contestant" to Western culture. Said, *Orientalism*, p.1. Simone de Beauvoir discusses the

uneasiness within British culture on both an internal and an external level. *Dracula* primarily deals with concerns surrounding the ethnic "other"; Stoker plays upon domestic phobias of imperial powers, such as Russia and its Slavic allies in the Balkans, to establish the foundation for the invasion of England by Count Dracula. Furthermore, he utilizes intertextuality to revive primal, agricultural-based fears of invasion by continental European powers. The sense of terror associated with the "other" is amplified by Stoker as he not only plays upon apprehensions about cultural differences, but also draws parallels to the subtle similarities between Britain's pre-industrial history and Transylvania's un-urbanized culture. James, however, focuses his narrative on internal social uneasiness with regards to gender and the "other". In particular, he explores the anxieties

---

gendered "other" as the female, with the notion of the white, Western man occupying the central position in society. de Beauvoir, *The Second Sex*, pp.xi–xii.

surrounding women entering the workplace and the impact of this on domestic power hierarchies. James uses his multi-layered narrative to blur the distinction between reality and the supernatural in his novella; the choice to focalize his narrative through the perceptions of the female "other" facilitates this confusion and allows for a greater sense of tension. These differing portrayals of the "other" suggest a strong sense of social apprehension towards the restructuring of British society, primarily caused by the aftermath of the Industrial Revolution and the Crimean War.[29] The greater mobility of capital, including the introduction of women into the labour force, and an increased phobia of the East, facilitated a period of change and anxieties associated with the ethnic and gendered "other".

Stoker creates an intricate perception of the ethnic "other" in *Dracula* and builds upon this

---

[29] Weightman, *The Industrial Revolution*, p.184, 265.

sense of differentiation to heighten the tension in his narrative, particularly between the protagonists and the Count. Jonathan Harker's journal is imbued with references to the differences between English and Transylvanian culture. These dissimilarities are initially benign, representing a mere inconvenience rather than a threat. For example, upon his arrival in the Carpathians, Harker remarks on the inconstant nature of the railway system: "It seems to me that the further East you go the more unpunctual are the trains".[30] He is repeatedly impressed by the local cuisine and notes that he should obtain the recipes for his fiancée; however, as he travels deeper into the East, he begins to find fault with the traditional dishes, likening them to animal food in London.[31] As his journey continues he becomes increasingly unsettled, particularly when

---

[30] Stoker, *Dracula*, p.11.

[31] Stoker, *Dracula*, pp.9–10. He likens "robber steak" to "London cat's-meat". Stoker, *Dracula*, p.13.

he first encounters the Slovaks, whom he describes as "the strangest figures we saw" and "more barbarian than the rest".[32] While waiting in a coach to journey to the Borgo Pass, Harker is viewed as an oddity amongst the various ethnic populations of Transylvania, as many of the peasants stare at him while he attempts to translate their remarks in his polyglot dictionary.[33] The emphasis in this encounter is not of fear or distrust amongst different ethnic groups; rather, it is of pity on the part of the peasants towards the unsuspecting foreigner.[34] Stoker provides an interesting interpretation of the perception of the "self" as viewed through the perspective of the "other". In this case, Harker is at an intellectual disadvantage as he can only view the emotions on the peasants' faces; he cannot interpret these

---

[32] Stoker, *Dracula,* p.11.

[33] Stoker, *Dracula,* p.13.

[34] Harker feels that they looked at him "pityingly". Stoker, *Dracula,* p.13.

signals, or communicate with the locals, as he lacks knowledge of the regional customs and languages.[35]

This tension between the "other" and the "self" is further heightened upon Harker's arrival at Dracula's castle. Harker feels out of place in the antiquated domestic setting. He attempts to locate a servant bell in order to inform the domestics that he has finished his meal; however, much to his astonishment, there is no bell available.[36] Harker reflects on this situation, stating: "There are certainly odd deficiencies in the house, considering the extraordinary evidences of wealth around me".[37] This suggests that Harker experiences a sense of both awe and

---

[35] Harker is a passive interpreter; he can only understand a few terrifying words, such as "Satan", "witch", "werewolf or vampire". Stoker, *Dracula*, p.13

[36] Stoker, *Dracula*, p.25.

[37] Stoker, *Dracula*, p.25.

confusion at his surroundings, contributing to Stoker's multi-layered construction of the differentiation between the "self" and the "other". The ethnic "other" is not portrayed as being inferior to the British "self", despite the evidence of industrial and technological "deficiencies"; rather, Stoker builds upon cultural differences to create a sense of uneasiness in the narrative. Harker gradually realizes that he is in danger, and that he has overlooked the various cultural warnings of the local peasants because of the dissimilarities between the two societies.[38]

The multiple references to the differences between British and Transylvanian culture serve as a basis for the introduction of Count Dracula into England, and heighten the sense of narrative

---

[38] For example, one peasant warns Harker of danger by forcing him to take her crucifix. Stoker, *Dracula*, p.13. Another warns him with gestures to ward off the evil eye. Stoker, *Dracula*, p.14.

tension between the "other" and the "self". The Count, who is the product of a society that lends itself to superstitions, is a destabilizing figure in industrial England. His command of wild animals, such as the wolf, appears grotesque in the streets of a modern city and causes chaos, whereas this same motif in the Count's native Romania adds to his sense of feudal dominance.[39] Stoker suggests that in the wild, un-urbanized Carpathians bestial predators respond to the superiority of the Count and that by introducing such a foreign terror into England, a systematized metropolis is reduced to chaos.[40] This mirrors the underlying anxiety within British culture of the dominance of Russian military power; although

---

[39] The Count refers to wolves as "the children of the night" and comments on Jonathan's obvious uneasiness at the presence of wild animals, "You dwellers in the city cannot enter into the feelings of the hunter". Stoker, *Dracula,* p.24.

[40] Stoker, *Dracula,* pp.125–6.

Russian technology was presumed to be inferior to that of the British, the overwhelming amount of human military capital was a source of anxiety for the British Empire.[41] Stoker's *Dracula* is fueled by this anxiety; the Count, who is the epitome of a feudal overlord, has the ability to replicate himself endlessly by creating additional vampires, just as the Russian Empire seemed to have a never-ending supply of soldiers.[42]

In emphasizing the role of the ethnic "other" as an invading force, Stoker subtly plays upon British suspicions of imperial Russia and post-Crimean War tensions, including Russia extending its influence into the Balkans.[43] Cain

---

[41] Cain, *Russophobia*, p.2; Royle, *Crimea*, p.7.

[42] Royle, *Crimea*, p.7.

[43] Russia stirred nationalist unrest in the Balkans after the Crimean War, claiming to be the champion of ethnic Slavs in the area. Ultimately, Russia took action against the Ottoman Empire and succeeded in granting many nations, such as Romania, their independence. Hupchick, *The Balkans*, pp.264–5.

suggests that this fear of Russia and its Slavic allies is quite overt in *Dracula*, employing the phrase "Russophobia".[44] However, such an argument neglects the subtle complexities of Stoker's concept of the "other", including Harker's impression of Eastern Europe and the role of Transylvanian peasants in defying the Count.[45] Harker, and Stoker by implication, is not as overtly xenophobic as Cain suggests.[46] Harker is impressed with the natural beauty of the

---

[44] Cain, *Russophobia*, pp.x, 14–15.

[45] For example, the various warnings the peasants give Harker about the Count. Stoker, *Dracula,* pp.13–4.

[46] Some of Harker's observations are racist, particularly within post-colonial criticism. For example, his reference to the Slavs as "barbarian". Stoker, *Dracula,* p.5. However, Harker does not display overt xenophobia as Cain suggests. For example, Cain describes Harker as having "deeply-held ethnic and cultural prejudices". Cain, *Russophobia*, p.144. Harker's language may also be influenced by a fear of pre-industrialized society.

unindustrialized countryside of the Carpathians and even likens the peasants to those of his native Britain. [47] In addition, it is the forethought of such Slavic peasants that spares Harker's life, via the gift of a crucifix necklace, when the Count is overwhelmed with bloodlust at the sight of Harker's exposed neck and shaving incision.[48] In doing this, Stoker suggests that the Count is a terror not only in London, but also amongst the various ethnic populations of the Carpathians.[49] Despite the high degree of Russophobia in Britain during the Victorian era, Cain over-amplifies this concept in his interpretation of Stoker's novel. Stoker uses the idea of the ethnic "other" to bridge the gap between the

---

[47] Stoker, *Dracula*, p.11.

[48] Stoker, *Dracula*, p.33.

[49] This concept is epitomized in the character of the grieving Transylvanian peasant mother, who futilely demands that the Count return her infant. Stoker, *Dracula*, pp.48–9.

supernatural and the rational, increasing the tension in the narrative surrounding the Count's introduction into England. The Count is a product of an un-urbanized, feudal culture, in which "every known superstition in the world is gathered", not unlike the pre-industrialized society of Britain.[50] Although elements of Russophobia exist in the text, Stoker's concept of the ethnic "other" is much more complicated than Cain suggests; it incorporates elements of Britain's feudal past to further fuel social anxiety, rather than being a purely xenophobic construction of the East.

Stoker's use of intertextuality, particularly with reference to superstitions, further accentuates his construction of anxieties towards the ethnic "other". Mina's account of Whitby, a coastal city in Yorkshire, mingles folklore and superstitions within an urbanized setting. Stoker's

---

[50] Stoker, *Dracula,* p.10.

various source texts, including historical narratives and poetry, are interwoven in Mina's description of the landscape and play upon its long history of invasion by foreign sources.[51] Her account of Whitby Abbey, which she describes as being "sacked by the Danes", is immediately annexed with the description of the local legend of a "white lady" who haunts it ruins. Stoker also combines Walter Scott's poem *Marmion* into this literary amalgamation, as Mina also references "the girl (who) was built up in the wall", referring to Constance de Beverley, who was bricked up in the abbey's cellar.[52] Mina questions a local inhabitant about the legend, whom she describes as being "a funny old man", in a parallel to Harker's encounter with the Slavic peasants in Transylvania.[53] The old man advises Mina not to become preoccupied with such stories; however,

---

[51] Stoker, *Dracula*, p.63.

[52] Stoker, *Dracula*, p.63.

[53] Stoker, *Dracula*, p.64.

he does not state that they are fictitious, but rather that they did not occur within his lifetime.[54] Stoker's description of Whitby, with its textual history of the supernatural and its association with foreign invasion, acts as a double for the Transylvanian countryside.[55] In doing this, Stoker links anxieties associated with invasion, superstition and the ethnic "other" within a single domestic space. In addition, Whitby is susceptible to supernatural forces because of its local myths and narratives arising from hauntings and brutal executions. Stoker's use of intertextuality, particularly his blending of historical and poetic

---

[54] Stoker, *Dracula,* p.64.

[55] Auerbach and Skal draw a parallel between Napoleon's invading forces and Dracula as an invader. Stoker, *Dracula,* p.64, footnote 7. Arata suggests that the decline of the British Empire further fueled the social anxiety of being "colonized by 'primitive' forces' in "a narrative of reverse colonization". Arata, "The Occidental Tourist", pp.621–3.

narratives, compounds the sense of anxiety towards the ethnic "other", as he emphasizes not only the differences between British and Slavic cultures, but also their subtle similarities.

Henry James' *The Turn of the Screw* shifts the focus of social anxiety from the national-level of the ethnic "other" to the microcosm of the household. The novella is contemporaneous with *Dracula* and post-dates Stoker's novel by only one year; however, it illustrates a marked difference in social concerns towards the domestic sphere and the presence of women, the gendered "other", in the workforce.[56] The wage-earning female is largely absent from *Dracula*, with the exception of Mina, who resembles a secretary as she diligently

---

[56] Most events in *The Turn of the Screw* are presumed to take place in the mid-nineteenth century as the narrator alludes to a forty-year difference between the actual events and the recounting of Douglas' story. James, *The Turn of the Screw*, p.3.

assists her husband by taking short-hand notes and typing his manuscripts, and also served as a teacher to Lucy.[57] Compared to Mina, the governess in *The Turn of the Screw* is an unstable counterpart, who ultimately ruins the children she is entrusted with protecting. This instability may be caused by a lack of socialization and anxiety associated with entering a new situation, as women of the Victorian age had limited employment opportunities.[58] Despite the

---

[57] Stoker, *Dracula,* p.55, 101.

[58] Hughes, *The Victorian Governess*, p.35. In one of the few instances in which the governess discusses her life prior to working at Bly house, she describes her existence as being "my small, smothered life", suggesting that she had very little contact with the world outside her home. James, *The Turn of the Screw*, p.14. The governess appears to be driven to enter the workforce because of unnamed domestic issues in her life. She mentions "disturbing letters from home" but does not elaborate on the issues. James, *The Turn of the Screw*, p.19.

economic growth of post-Industrial Revolution England, women had access to relatively few professions, the role of governess, or that of a domestic servant, being amongst them.[59] These limitations placed on women in the workforce led to a significant disparity in income between the sexes and is often demonstrated in Gothic narratives by the dependence of the female characters on a male figure for their livelihood.

This uneven distribution of wealth in the Victorian age complicated the hierarchy of women within the working sphere, as is evident in the relationship between the governess and Mrs. Grose. The governess, who was of a slightly higher economic station than a housekeeper, dominates Mrs. Grose in matters of household importance, which later incorporate the issues of

---

[59] Hughes, *The Victorian Governess*, pp.4, 30, 35.

the supernatural.[60] Initially, the subtle power dynamic is evident in the interactions between the two women. The governess causes Mrs. Grose to feel uneasy about her lack of education and about the implied neglect of Miles, which may have contributed to his permanent dismissal from school.[61] As her visions of the dead intensify, the governess is able to convince Mrs. Grose of the presence of the supernatural despite the housekeeper's initial reservations. After a mild interrogation regarding her vision of Miss Jessel, Mrs. Grose quickly reverses her skeptical position and begins to enable the governess's delusions.[62] The governess describes Mrs. Grose as initially

---

[60] James emphasizes the importance of the generous income in the narrator's choice to take the role: "The salary offered much exceeded her modest measure". James, *The Turn of the Screw*, p.5. For the domestic social hierarchy, see Peterson, *The Victorian Governess*, p.13.

[61] James, *The Turn of the Screw*, p.10.

[62] James, *The Turn of the Screw*, pp.29–31.

"not too bewildered instinctively to protest";
however, she is soon swayed by the governess's
description of Miss Jessel and begins to fill in the
deficiencies of her story.[63] Mrs. Grose's lack of
education and her lower position in the domestic
hierarchy contribute to her submissive nature
with respect to the governess. Generally, a
Victorian governess was not in an overt position
of power with regards to servants such as
housekeepers; however, there was an implied
domestic rank, as the servants were expected to
attend to the governess as well as guests and
other household members.[64] James accentuates
this subtle power struggle, creating tension
between the two characters. This suggests that
the architecture of the female "other" in his

---

[63] James, *The Turn of the Screw*, p.30.

[64] Peterson further discusses the sense of resentment
towards the typical Victorian governess by the other
servants attributed to the domestic hierarchy.
Peterson, *The Victorian Governess*, p.13.

novella is intricate; the politics of sex within the working environment are not only complicated by higher wage earning men, but also by differences in female stations within the middle-class.

The nineteenth century sense of female identity, complicated by social perceptions of the working-class woman, affects James' construction of the female narrator and gives voice to the typically marginalized "other". James uses the device of the homodiegetic first-person narrator to convey the governess's account of her story in her own words.[65] He embeds this narrative within two broader narratives: the reading of the manuscript by Douglas, which is in turn embedded within the story of an unknown narrator. Although this narrative device can have a distancing effect on the dialogue of the "other", James reiterates the importance of recounting the

---

[65] Newman, "Getting Fixed: Female Identity", p.45.

events in the governess's own words. This is achieved by having Douglas insist on reading from the manuscript, rather than relating the story from memory, despite the protestations of his peers.[66] In doing this, James gives voice to a marginalized member of Victorian society, and does not attempt to rationalize or filter the voice by paraphrasing it through a male figure. Rather, Douglas attests to the severity of the narrative; he states, "It's beyond everything. Nothing at all that I know touches it". Furthermore, the initial narrator, whom James has purposefully left genderless, copies the manuscript as "an exact transcript", intensifying the desire to maintain the dialogue of the female "other".[67] These extra

---

[66] James, *The Turn of the Screw*, p.2.

[67] James, *The Turn of the Screw*, p.4. While the sex of the ultimate narrator is never divulged, there is a strong tradition of "reading masculinity" into the role. Newman attempts to "feminize" the narrator by examining the language in relation to the feminine gaze; however, she ultimately concludes that it is

"layers" of narrative authority are required given the historical context of the text. The working-class Victorian female was subject to an intense level of social scrutiny; women were perceived to be at the mercy of their fantastical imaginations and often susceptible to insanity.[68] By including the additional levels of narrators, and having both attest to the importance of the voice of the "other", James constructs an important dialogue for the generally marginalized working-class female.

The historical perceptions regarding female insanity, fueled by the social belief that women were prone to being overcome by their "imaginations", facilitates the blurring effect between reality and the supernatural in the narrative. This ambiguity with regards to the

---

impossible to determine the gender, as the narrator lends itself to a reading of either sex. Newman, "Getting Fixed: Female Identity", pp.45–7.

[68] Porter, *Madness*, p.87.

limits of the governess's reality has stimulated academic debate concerning the definition of her mental state. Newman suggests that the governess displays signs of madness, particularly in relation to her fixation with the fate of Miss Jessel. James employs the Gothic motif of being "haunted by residues of the past"; in this instance, the governess is preoccupied with the death of her predecessor, a "lady" as Mrs. Grose defines her, who reduced her social standing by associating with Peter Quint.[69] Wilson's Freudian reading of the text emphasizes the splintered nature of the governess's mind and suggests that the ghosts are a product of the pathologized obsessions of a "spinster".[70] Such debates neglect to examine the impact of the governess upon Douglas, who, despite the large passage of time

---

[69]James, *The Turn of the Screw*, pp.31–2. For the theme of being haunted by the past, see Punter, *The Gothic*, p.123.

[70] Wilson, "The Ambiguity of Henry James", p.173.

since his encounter with her, is still noticeably affected by her story. Douglas provides proof that the governess was never deemed to be mad; she went on to become the instructor of his sister. He furthermore describes her as "the most agreeable woman I've ever known in her position; she'd have been worthy of any whatever".[71]

Veeder's reading suggests a possible explanation for these inconsistencies: the governess's oppressed hostility towards her father is replicated in her new domestic setting and transferred to the other male characters in the text, the master of Bly house and Miles.[72] The lack of an appropriate outlet for this frustration towards the new patriarchal structure contributes to her already nervous mental state.[73] The

---

[71] James, *The Turn of the Screw*, p.2.

[72] Veeder, "The Nurturance of the Gothic", pp.81–2.

[73] The governess is described as being apprehensive about her new role: "…the prospect struck her as

governess, who was the daughter of a "poor country parson", arrives in London with little knowledge of the metropolitan world, and is overwhelmed during her first encounter with her employer.[74] The large absence of the employer from the remainder of the narrative leads to a complication in her relationship with Miles, as he assumes the position of the key male character in the text. Miles' adult-like demeanor, and the governess's reaction to this, suggests that she transposes part of her oppressed emotions onto

---

slightly grim. She was young, untried, nervous: it was a vision of serious duties and little company, of really great loneliness". James, *The Turn of the Screw*, p.5.

[74] James, *The Turn of the Screw*, p.4. The disparity in economic status between the impoverished governess and her employer may have further contributed to her sense of transferred hostility, as her employer was in a position of patriarchal power as the head of Bly house. The ultimate manifestation of this latent hostility is her role in the death of Miles. Veeder, "The Nurturance of the Gothic", p.68.

the child, further complicating her already anxious state.[75] By creating an intricate psychological dimension to the narrator, James amplifies the lack of awareness surrounding the complexity of female psychology within the Victorian age, a source of social anxiety and tension in the text. The choice to focalize the narrative through the viewpoint of the gendered "other" facilitates a sense of confusion between the supernatural and the psychological, as the marginalized figure of the female, middle-class woman was often assumed to be on the verge of insanity.[76] James complicates this underlying social anxiety as he repeatedly suggests that the governess is able to continue to function in her profession after the events at Bly house. This is significant, particularly given the propensity of Victorian medical professionals to have women

---

[75] Veeder, "The Nurturance of the Gothic", p.67.

[76] Porter, *Madness*, p.87.

committed for the slightest display of mental instability.[77]

Gothic narratives are imbued with references to the "other", be it in the form of the ethnic "other", such as in Stoker's *Dracula*, or the gendered "other", as in James' *The Turn of the Screw*. This emphasis on the "other", in opposition to the "self", creates tension in the underlying narratives by drawing upon social anxieties at both the macro and micro social levels. *Dracula* emphasizes the cultural differences and subtle similarities between Victorian Britain and feudal Transylvania. Stoker's construction of the ethnic "other" fuses political apprehensions about the rise of the Russian Empire, and its influence upon southern Slavs, with fears of invasion by continental European forces. Intertextuality is used to draw upon superstitions in historical narratives and poetry, conveying a

---

[77] Porter, *Madness*, p.87.

sense of Britain's feudal past, not unlike that of the Count's Transylvania. James uses a complex construction of the working middle-class female "other" to create tension in the Victorian household, ultimately resulting in the destruction of the children under the governess's charge. The use of a multilayered narrative structure, coupled with the dominance of the female "other" in the text, allows for a greater sense of confusion about the boundaries between the supernatural and reality. The prevalence of the "other" in these Gothic narratives suggests multiple underlying social anxieties during the Victorian age, reflecting a period of complexity and cultural change in which the attitudes towards foreigners and women were continually expressed in literature.

Bibliography

Primary Texts

James, H., *The Turn of the Screw* ed. Deborah Esch
and Jonathan Warren (London & New   York:
W.W. Norton & Company, 1999).

Stoker, B., *Dracula* ed. Nina Auerbach and David
J. Skal (London & New York: W.W. Norton &
Company, 1997).

Secondary Texts

Arata, S. D., "The Occidental Tourist: *Dracula*
and the Anxiety of Reverse Colonization"

Victorian Studies 33 no.4 (summer, 1990) pp.621–45.

Cain, J.E., *Bram Stoker and Russophobia: Evidence of the British Fear of Russia in Dracula and The Lady of the Shroud* (Jefferson: McFarland & Company Inc., 2006).
de Beauvoir, S., *The Second Sex* trans. M. Parshley (New York: Vintage Books, 1989).

Hughes, K., *The Victorian Governess* (London: The Hambledon Press, 1993).

Hupchick, D.P., *The Balkans: From Constantinople to Communism* (New York: Palgrave, 2001).

Newman, B., "Getting Fixed: Feminine Identity and Scopic Crisis in 'The Turn of the Screw'" NOVEL: A Forum on Fiction 26 no.1 (autumn, 1992) pp.43–63.

Peterson, M.J., "The Victorian Governess: Status Incongruence in Family and Society" in Martha Vicinus ed. *Suffer and Be Still: Women in the Victorian Age* (London: Methuen & Co. Ltd, 1980) pp.3–19.

Porter, R., *Madness: A Brief History* (Oxford: Oxford University Press, 2002).

Royle, T., *Crimea: The Great Crimean War, 1854–1856* (New York: Palgrave Macmillan 2000).

Said, E.W., *Orientalism* (New York: Random House Inc., 1979).

Veeder, W., "The Nurturance of the Gothic: 'The Turn of the Screw'" *Gothic Studies* 1 no.1 (1999) pp.47–85.

Weightman, G., *The Industrial Revolutionaries: The Making of the Modern World 1776– 1914* (New York: Grove Atlantic, 2007).

Wilson, E., "The Ambiguity of Henry James" in Henry James *The Turn of the Screw* ed. Deborah Esch and Jonathan Warren (London & New York: W.W. Norton & Company, 1999).

ABOUT THE AUTHOR

Marija grew up in a delicatessen, with a multiethnic family, where pickling cabbage and knife throwing were taught at an early age. She would scribble stories on butcher's paper that would then be passed on to unsuspecting customers when they received their groceries.

She is the recipient of numerous academic awards from the University of Sydney, including the 2011 Senior Essay Prize in Classics, the Dean's Merit Award, and the Walter Reid Memorial prize.

She lives in Sydney with her husband (*el carnicero*), her daughter, and a bunch of pirate pets.

www.marijaelektrarodriguez.com

www.ingramcontent.com/pod-product-compliance
Lightning Source LLC
Chambersburg PA
CBHW030938150426
42812CB00064B/3032/J